MEMOIR

AND

IN MEMORIAM

OF

HENRY TRAVIS, M.D.,

BY

E. T. CRAIG.

Memoir and In Memoriam

OF

HY. TRAVIS, M.D.,

ENGLISH SOCIALIST,

AND AUTHOR OF

"Free Will and Law in Perfect Harmony," "Moral Freedom and Causation," "Effectual Reform in Man and Society," "The Co-operative System of Society," "English Socialism," "A Manual of Social Science," &c., &c.

HIS WORK AND CHARACTER.

By E. T. CRAIG, of Ralahine.

With CRITIQUE by Dr. EADON.

Co-operative Printing Society Limited, 17, Balloon-street, Corporation-street, Manchester.

MR. CRAIG AND THE LATE DR. TRAVIS.

THE following critique on the "Memoir" and "In Memoriam" of the late Dr. TRAVIS is interesting, as Dr. EADON accepts the doctrines of Dr. GALL as the true philosophy of Mind and Character, which Mr. CRAIG has for so many years earnestly advocated, as the most important, practical, and useful knowledge to be made known to mankind. The position of Dr. EADON is one of high standing among his professional brethren, as shown by this month's statement in the *Journal of Medicine and Dosimetric Therapeutics*, under the editorship of Dr. PHIPSON, where it is stated that the Institute of Dosimetric Medicine, of Paris, has awarded to Dr. EADON its Diploma of Honour, which runs thus:—"In consideration of the remarkable interest and eminent services rendered to the Dosimetric method by Dr. SAMUEL EADON, the Institute of Dosimetric Medicine, of Paris, in testimony of high esteem and gratitude, decrees in general assembly, held in Paris, 54, Rue de Francs Bourgeois, a Diploma of Honour, and in faith to him we decree the present testimonial.

"A. BURGGRAEVE, Prof., President.

"CHARLES CHANTEAUD, Pharmaceutist.

"Paris, March 18th, 1884."

To E. T. Craig, Esq , the Historian of Ralahine, and the last living member of the first-formed band of the great co-operative movement.

Hambrook Court, near Bristol, April 15, 1884.

My dear sir,—I have read, in the *Co-operative News*, of April 12, with considerable interest the loving tribute and death-lament of your friend and coadjutor, Dr. Henry Travis, and likewise your touching lines on his life-work, as given, with softened cadence, in your " In Memoriam." The co-operative societies of Great Britain will, doubtless, feel proud that one old " gnarled oak " still stands " amidst a forest growth of younger trees " the symbol of bygone years of vigorous life ; that the " old man eloquent," with his hoary locks of more than four score winters, still lives to move his magic pen, and do honour to his fellow compeers who pass off, one by one, from the duties and responsibilities of earth-life, to a higher, nobler, and grander form of being. Yes, it is glorious to sit and listen, how the cerebral harp sounds responsive to the spirit fingers still evoking music sweet and pleasant, and it is charming to think of, and muse over, how,

> A harp of a thousand strings
> Has kept in tune so long.

But so it is. Thanks, a thousand thanks for the length of life bestowed.

The sketch given of your friend Dr. Travis is, doubtless, an encomium of his talents and virtues, but yet it is discriminating and true. Standing on the cerebral rock of the illustrious Gall, you command a wider horizon, and perceive objects which cannot come within the range of the mental telescope of those occupying a less elevated position, whether they be the French Helvetius, or the Lanarkshire Owen, or the co-operating advocate, Travis. With you, genius is something more than the result of " favourable outward circumstances," and society, in its growth and interweavements, the resultant of causes other than those of objective phenomena, and of that metaphysical nonentity THE WILL, a faculty without an organ by which to manifest itself, unless the whole brain, in its whole entirety of action, concentrated to one point, object, or circumstance, is considered as the unific organ of The Will ; if so, then, to Will-Power much action must, of necessity, be ascribed. But if this be correct, even in a limited extent, the philosophy of its action on society must be misty, and often of doubtful result. The principle advocated by you—that the brain is the organ of the mind, and that every faculty or power of the human spirit has a corresponding cerebral organ, whereby it is manifested, undoubtedly lies at the foundation of all advancement, whether individually, or socially, and although, as you say, Robert Owen, and your friend, Dr. Travis, " were made acquainted with these views, and admitted the principle,

yet, it is uncertain whether they apprehended their full practical consequences, as both fail to dwell on it (the cerebral philosophy of mind)
in the exposition of their advanced views." Standing as you always have
done on the rock of cerebral truth, I congratulate you, that, at this late
period of life, and with knees less vigorous than of yore, the waves of
friendship have been powerless to wash you off. For it was neither
"outward circumstances" nor "Will-Power" which caused Dr. Travis
to take such a deep and abiding interest in the educational efforts of
Robert Owen, or in the great social co-operative movement which he so
long helped to foster and promote; but, in his fine Cerebral Organisation,
with its expansive moral lobes, and intellectual front, with its deep
cineritious depositions. From this, and this alone, resulted the
actions of his life—a life that won your love, and makes you say—

No pang in social life like that which breaks
The heart-strings holding fast true friends :
And mine now bleeds at ev'ry broken chord
Of sympathy and love.

Your friend was clearly one of Nature's noblemen. His aim was to
do good, to establish social co-operation, and "drive out from society
the gnawing cancer of competition." Hence his numerous writings
and his constant labours to benefit in every way his fellows. He was
a model man ; and the tear of friendship dropt upon his grave, and
the immortelles of love so conspicuously placed by you before his
wide circle of friends in loving memory, are honourable to both; the
one, as being worthy of such a tribute, the other, as having the power
to record, in language, the goodness of his own heart. "A good man
died when Travis passed away" says your "In Memoriam," but his
deeds of goodness will live for ever. He heard "the workers' wail of
woe ;" he knew the tyranny of wealth; the slavery of the working
class ; the theft of land, the common gift of God to all ; the wage-
competition of man with man ; the greater the wealth, the deeper goes
the steel of slavery into the heart of man ; and that landlordism and
capital are the damning curses of modern life—these he knew, and to
uncoil the chain of slavery from the toiling millions, he moved heart,
and brain, and hand, to the utmost of his power, but in vain. The
day, however, will come when the white slaves of civilisation will—

. . . . Madly take the law
With vengeful fury into their own hands,
. . . . And with blood
Wash out the title-deeds of lands now kept
As hunting grounds for wild and useless game,
For drones who live on honey gathered by
The starving workers famishing for food.

In a few lines, you have written quite a little treatise on the land
question ; summed up the excellences of your friend, now showing his
love for Robert Owen's work, and next, his hatred of land-theft and

the consequent present bound-down condition of the working, and still, poorer classes ; and, in conclusion, with a fan-fare of trumpets, you boldly proclaim the convictions of a life's study, and practical testing on thousands of heads, that the spirit of man can only be known in this life as it manifests itself through its organ the brain ; and, in spite of all the metaphysics of Cudworth, Reid, Stewart, Brown, and a whole host of similar writers, you dare to say :—

> While science demonstrates the truth and power
> Of that great law which proves the brain,
> The source of mental force, and gives each faculty
> Its separate organ, varying forms
> Of size and quality, each with its own
> Just means of satisfaction ; thus the brain
> Becomes as readable as other forms
> Throughout the visible wide universe.

Wishing you improved health, with the coming genial warmth of the season.—Believe me, faithfully yours,

SAMUEL EADON, M.A , M.D., Ph.D., &c.
Of the Universities of Edinburgh, Glasgow, and Aberdeen.

CHARACTER IS FORMED BY THE COMBINED ACTION OF
EXTERNAL CONDITIONS OR CIRCUMSTANCES,
AND INTERNAL IMPULSES AWAKENED
BY THEIR NATURAL STIMULI.

DR. TRAVIS.

HIS WORK AND CHARACTER.

"GONE BEFORE."

THE demise of HENRY TRAVIS, M.D., is a sad and severe loss to the great social co-operative movement, which he has so long helped to foster and promote. He passed away to join the great majority on the 4th of February, at seventy-seven years of age, and was interred at Finchley on Friday, the 8th of February. He held a conspicuous position as the literary executor of ROBERT OWEN, the founder of social science and co-operation. He was one of three of the "Old Guard," who were identified with the socialistic aspect of co-operation beginning in Manchester in 1827. Dr. TRAVIS belonged to a family of physicians, who for three generations have been in practise in Scarborough. His father and grandfather were well-known to the aristocratic visitors of this queen of watering places on the Yorkshire coast. The mental and moral characteristics of Dr. TRAVIS led him, naturally, to take a deep and abiding interest in the educational efforts of ROBERT OWEN, and to sympathise with his successful training of the young at New Lanark—a success realised without the old methods of reward and corporal punishment, rivalry, place-taking, and the excitement of evil passions. The extraordinarily success-ful and happy results on the rising generation had attracted the attention of leading philanthropists, politicians, and some of the crowned heads of Europe. The Duke of KENT, father of Queen VICTORIA, sent his physician, Dr. MACNAB, to examine into Mr. OWEN's plans, and published the report after a fort-night's residence. So satisfied was the duke with the account, that he arranged with Mr. OWEN to allow him to bring his family for a brief residence at Braxfield House, the residence of ROBERT OWEN, but the death of the duke frustrated the design.

The Grand Duke NICHOLAS (afterwards the Emperor of Russia) visited New Lanark, and, after examining the schools and watching the cheerful exercises of the children, he invited Mr. OWEN to St. Petersburg to establish similar schools in Russia, and promised every assistance required. Men like JEREMY BENTHAM, HENRY BROUGHAM, and WILLIAM ALLEN, took a practical interest and invested capital in Mr. OWEN's plans with much profit.

Mr. OWEN, with fervid enthusiasm, held that the successful training of the young was the necessary effect of his doctrine of circumstances in the formation of character, which led many to study his writings and to visit the scene of his labours. Among others who studied the published works of the great and successful manufacturer of cotton yarns and the marvellous moulder of men and children was Dr. TRAVIS, who became deeply interested, and sympathised with the efforts of the great philathropist, and ultimately became a favourite disciple, and joined in one or two of his plans. He was one of the residents at Titherley farm, and while he regretted the failure of the scheme, he attributed the disappointment to the want of capital, and in part to the unsuitable soil rather than to moral causes. He became from that time more active than before in advocating social co-operation through the medium of the press, and on the death of Mr. OWEN, he became his literary executor.

In 1851-2-3 Dr. TRAVIS was editor of *Robert Owen's Journal*, published weekly, at a penny, and in volumes at 2s. 6d. each. The motto on vol. IV., for 1852, runs thus :—

" The Character of Man is formed *for* him ; and not *by* him."
[Except as a *caused* agent]

The sub-clause in brackets, with the word emphasised by italics, and without quotation commas, was doubtless added by the editor, and clearly indicates the time when Dr. TRAVIS began to see the necessity of analysing and qualifying Mr. OWEN's dogma as to the doctrine of circumstances in the development of character.

The thorough knowledge possessed by Dr. TRAVIS of Mr. OWEN's views, both from personal intercourse and his writings, made him well qualified for a critical examination of his master's philosophy. While admitting the great work he had done, as originator of social science, he differed from Mr. OWEN in his statement that man's determinations are, in all cases, "formed for him, and not by him;" or, in other words, that man is not an agent in the forming of his determinations, which is to imagine that man has no power or agency in causing his acts—for his acts are effects of his determinations. And to have no power or agency in causing of action would be to have no power of self-control. To have no power of self-control is to be insane or imbecile. But to say that man's determination is dependent upon conditions, is to assert a truth of very great importance —the truth which is asserted in the true part of the common idea of philosophic necessity, and which is denied in the erroneous part of the common notion of free will.

This investigation led Dr. TRAVIS to modify his views as to the irresistible power of external conditions, and while admitting their influence and force in education, contended that culture and training would enable a man to still further react or resist certain impulses arising from his internal conditions or state of mind. This difference between the pupil and the master is of vital importance. With Mr. OWEN man acts from the necessity of his constitution. The principles on which he managed New Lanark were thus briefly embodied :

1. Man does not form his own character : it is formed for him by the circumstances that surround him.

2. Man is not a fit subject of praise or blame.

3. Any general character, good or bad, may be given to the world by applying means which are to a great extent under the control of human governments.

Dr. TRAVIS holds that man is influenced both by external conditions or circumstances, as in educational training, and also by internal conditions enabling his "Will" to carry out his determinations. Therefore man is responsible for his actions caused by his determinations.

Dr. TRAVIS considers that "Mr. OWEN's views were taught in an injurious manner, and falsified, and impossible to be explained and practically applied, and were the most important knowledge which has been discovered in the history of the human race."

It will be seen that Dr. TRAVIS has achieved a great and noble task in analysing fundamental truths so as to give an entirely different reading and meaning to the metaphysical terms necessary to teach true social science. It is only by the knowledge of the causes which propel to action and to form character that man can be enabled to acquire enlightened goodness which is necessary for the realisation of a well-ordered and happy state of society.

To this statement may be added the important truth that both Dr. TRAVIS and ROBERT OWEN would have gained immensely in practical skill had the great truths that are involved in the fact that every faculty of the brain has a special organ allotted to the manifestation of its function, and the size, quality, and culture of the organ corresponds with its power of manifestation.

This law is as certain and uniform as the truths of mathematics or morality, and each faculty has its proper objects to arouse its innate activity, as the presence of dangerous fire awakens fear. There are men who cannot tell the difference between the tune of "God Save the Queen" and the "Old Hundredth" psalm. Other men may be met with who are idiots in one or more faculties, when the brain is below the average size in certain organs. The higher sentiments may manifest themselves freely when the organs are large and active, while those giving energy may be absent, when feebleness will be the result, whatever may be the outward conditions. An idiot can never be made into a philosopher. ROBERT OWEN was made acquainted with these views, and while he subsequently admitted the principle involved, it is very doubtful if he apprehended the practical consequences, Dr. TRAVIS, in his conversation with me, admitted the principle as to the relation between organisation, capability, and character, although he fails to dwell on it in the exposition of his advanced views.

English socialism in theory is the science of society. This science is the knowledge which must be obtained before men can acquire the enlightened character necessary to know and apply, or become an important part of the combination of influences—in persons, ideas, and surroundings. This science of society was discovered and practically verified by ROBERT OWEN. But it could not be clearly explained by its discoverer, because it is based upon a truth which requires for its completion to be combined with another truth in relation to the formation of character, in capacity, and conduct by educational training. This error is now corrected by Dr. TRAVIS and made intelligible.

The result of these views held by Dr. TRAVIS would realise "an improved state of society in a system of social co-operation attained by self-supporting social arrangements, in which permanent, useful, and well-remunerated employments will be provided for the working classes; first, under influences most favourable to their improvement and happiness, at once economical and beautiful in construction for those who are now in poverty and want of employment. These arrangements will be gradually developed and made still more attractive for those who are in more favoured circumstances. The interest for the capital employed in these new arrangements will be provided for by the surplus productions of the associations."

To realise these views of Dr. TRAVIS will require a wiser use of profits of trade than are at present evident, and it may require an agency of propaganda more effective than yet established. It will require something like a moral avalanche to extinguish the errors of centuries before the quiet truths of social co-operation can drive out the gnawing cancer of competition. A federation of funds, or one-half the yearly profits—say, one million sterling per annum, with spare share capital—would provide ample means for great and marvellous success, with gratifying results both in social economy and happiness.

Dr. TRAVIS is the author of several admirable works on social reform, such as "Effectual Reform," "Free Will and Law," "Moral Freedom Reconciled with Causation," published by LONGMAN and Co. "English Socialism," published by A. HEYWOOD, Manchester, and the Guild of Co-operators, pp. 88, price 3d. per post. This is the most popular work of Dr. TRAVIS, and deserves the attention of all social co-operators. "A Manual of Social Science," price 6½d., is published by JOHN HEYWOOD. He has contributed numerous valuable papers to quarterly, monthly, and weekly magazines, but we have not space here to refer to them. He was most orderly, punctual, and painstaking, and a marvel of industry in arranging the articles in portfolios which he devised. On one occasion he showed me his journals (several of which I now possess), made by his own hands, filled with copies of his articles published in various magazines. I told him I had hundreds of columns which I had written in journals of which I had been editor, but I had never found time to paste many in journals as I had intended. To show me his method of working he fetched from his bedroom a thick journal, 9in. by 7in., and 1in. thick, of ruled pages, filled with the original compositions of his articles, as the thoughts had occurred to him when awake in the night. He had a bracket at the head of his bed on which he kept a benzoline lamp ready to be lighted, on awaking in the night, when he would resume his studies, and jot down his thoughts as they arose, and afterwards would correct and revise them, and hence his pages were crowded with fastidious corrections, interlineations, and marginal revisions. At my next visit he presented me with a new note book, and also an ingenious pencil of the "Eagle" patent, which had just been brought from America by a nephew of Dr. TRAVIS. The journal I prize, and the pencil has done good service in drafting this, too brief, memoir.

The death of Dr. TRAVIS is a great loss to the cause of human progress, and his memory is lovingly cherished by his large circle of friends. He was greatly esteemed for his high and lofty moral tone of character. He had a noble presence, and an expression ever beaming with sympathy, kindness, charity, and benevolence. Those who possess his portrait can

See what grace was seated on this brow.

A combination and a form indeed,
Where every good deed seems to set its seal
To give the world assurance of a man.

I have known many good men, and have delineated many thousands of characters, both in public and in private life, but two of the noblest and best of men I have intimately known were the great Socialists, Dr. TRAVIS and ROBERT OWEN. Both were alike honourable, generous, and courteous towards others, never speaking disparagingly of other men, but charitably ascribing errors, and even vicious habits, to the influence of heritage and adverse external conditions, rather than to innate tendencies and vicious dispositions. Perhaps they carried these views a little beyond historic facts, for society may breed criminals, as it developes goitre and other low organisms. There is practical philosophy in this truth in relation to the future evolution of higher phases of humanity.

There was a quiet dignity in our friend's manner, united to a modesty that was neither shrinking humility nor feeble weakness. Had I not known him intimately, I might have viewed his even-balanced character as evidence of negative qualities, but his gentleness was the effect of his philosophic convictions prompting him to a charitable consideration of the feelings and conduct of others. He once spoke with emphasis, force, and indignation, against a writer who had misrepresented ROBERT OWEN and other well-known pioneers, and for a moment was as a lion roused to energy of action. He was fond of studious retirement, and avoided all public displays and noisy agitations.

In November last, in reply to my communications, my friend sent me a post-card with the following few pregnant words :—" So much pain—I cannot write more."

From that time, till the closing scene, his sufferings (from calculus) must have been very severe and excruciating, although he had intervals of ease, but he clearly foresaw the end.

He was very regular, temperate, and abstemious in his habits. I frequently joined him at a social cup of tea, but he always limited himself to new milk, and whole meal, or white bread. Mr. OWEN was alike temperate, and abstemious, as I often saw him take a basin of warm milk and bread at his breakfast and at his supper. These men were noble

examplers, both in their lives and in their closing scenes in
death, and we—who must soon follow them—should rejoice
at the great good they accomplished rather than grieve
that they have yielded to the inevitable, although it is
difficult to subdue the feelings under sincere, heartfelt
sorrow by mere cold argument. Severed affections know
nothing of logical syllogisms. A tear dropped on the grave
of a dear departed friend becomes the proudest potentate as
it does the humblest of affectionate hearts, and the finest
wreath of *immortelles* we can give them is to imitate their best
and noblest attributes. There was only one Dr. TRAVIS, and

We shall never see his like again.

3, Andover-road, Hammersmith.   E. T. CRAIG

In Memoriam of

HENRY TRAVIS, M.D.,

WHO DIED 4th FEBRUARY, 1884, ÆTAT 77.

By E. T. CRAIG.

Not for himself he lived, but for his race.

OLD friends, like autumn leaves, are falling fast
   In life's great battle.   Death soon conquers all!
   And now, when four score years have come and gone,
   Alone I seem to stand, a gnarlèd oak,
   Amidst a forest growth of fruitless trees;
   The last of that small group—a social host,
     Of Owen,* Thompson,† Morgan ‡ Finch § and Pare, ‖
And now one joins the great majority
Who asks us " not to grieve, but rather still
Rejoice, the weary travellers' at rest."

   A good man died when Travis passed away;
With silent fortitude he suffered long:
Now pain and sorrow are for him no more.

   No pang in social life like that which breaks
The heart-strings holding fast true friends;
And mine now bleeds at ev'ry broken chord
Of sympathy and love, full soon to reach
The same dark pathway to the tomb.
The heart now throbs and feels its loss the more

---

* Robert Owen, founder of infant schools, social science, and mutual co-operation. † William Thompson, author of " The Distribution of Wealth." ‡ John Minter Morgan, author of " Revolt of the Bees." " Brutus," &c. § John Finch, author of " Letters on Ralahine." ‖ William Pare, author of " Capital and Labour."

By reason of his pallid, speechless corse,
In one long, everlasting sleep.

How like to dreamless sleep is thoughtless death !
Although the mortal dies the spirit lives,
And ever passes through the perfumed flowers
Where birds will sip the dew-drop from the leaves—
Ascending high to chant his requiem
In thrilling notes of sweetness and of joy,
Eternal through the ages yet to come.

The vital force has fled, and he is gone
Who made life precious to a loving heart.
His thoughts and work shall live—and like the stars
That guide the mariner o'er trackless seas,
To where he finds his haven, home, and rest,
In peace, content, and happy days of joy.
His gentle life was one long scene of peace,
Where passion had no part to play in life,
Which taught a cheerfulness in duty, faith
In kindly human nature, as men err
Through lack of knowledge of the laws of mind—
Of motives swaying action—diff'ring from
His teacher's creed and "fundamental law,"
Which holds that outward circumstances rule
The inward instincts, so that " character
Was made *for* man not *by* himself " alone ;
Hence outward influence made vice and crime !

He loved to dwell on Owen's noblest work
Of moulding youthful minds to virtuous deeds :
Who raised the lowly, and aroused the dull
To efforts, without fear or dread of pain,
Or punishment for lack of genius.
He proved the world mistaken in belief,
That all mankind were made to feel and act
From innate viciousness of heart, and shows
By facts that education makes the man
A monster or a minister of peace ;
While prizes freely shower'd on nature's gifts

Will cultivate a sordid jealous greed,
For what is moral poison to the man
Who fails to reach the prizeman's post.

    Our friend would own the power of circumstance—
That wealth or poverty would guide the hand,
And prompt the heart to good or evil deeds,
And aggravate the agony of wrong.
And thus he heard the worker's wail of woe :—

    " Hear ye not the secret sighing ?
        And the tear drops thro' the night—
    See ye not a nation dying
        For want of food, and air, and light ? "

    From Orient lands there came the bitter cry
Of millions toiling in the scorching sun,
To raise the crops that others reap as rent,
From bounteous nature's thankfulness to toil,
Yet leave the ryot starving for the food,
As thus he wails in doleful misery :—

    " Oh God ! I can endure no more
        This crushing load of tax and toil ;
    Is this the curse of being poor—
        The curse on those who till the soil ?
    " Ah me ! it is a fearful life
        To know no hope, no gleam of joy—
    To wage a sharp eternal strife
        With ills that flesh and soul destroy !
" Strike hard the turf, or drive the ploughshare deep,
And sow, that Wealth your harvests all may reap !

    " Breathe I beneath free Albion's sway ?
        The helot's bonds too well I feel ;
    A hundred years have passed away,
        Yet sink I deeper, deeper still !
    The law but rivets fast my chain ;
        Each year but forges shackles new.
    Oh, Albion, count thy glorious gain—
        A people ruined for a few ?

" Strike hard the turf, oh drive the ploughshare deep,
And sow, that Wealth your harvests all may reap !"

He grieved to think these sufferings needless, for,
He knew that labour multiplied the wealth,
By aid of steam and force, a thousand fold,
Abstracted now in profits from good men ;
While ev'ry rood of habitable soil,
Is claimed by force of might, and laws
Enacted by the grabbing few, while all
Poor wage-paid men are made the slaves of toil—
In competition with each other slave.

II.

The day will come when men made desperate
Will blindly yield and madly take the law,
With vengeful fury, into their own hands—
With blazing torch will one wide ruin make
For those who shout—" Each look to himself alone
The devil take the poorest !"   Then will blood
Wash out the title-deeds of lands now kept
As hunting grounds for wild and useless game,
For drones who live on honey gathered by
The starving workers famishing for food,
While all might wealthy be, if each would share
In work, and gather in the harvest of the land,
So prodigal of riches held for those
Who give their labour to enjoy the fruit.

Thus Travis saw man poor from lack of thought,
And aimed to form the means to change the scene
To one of reason, justice, kindness, truth,
In motive, word and deed, so that he might
Reform men's minds, like clay on potter's wheel,
To shapes of beauty, use, and ornament.

This truth he taught, that outward forces had
Their influence while inward impulse gave,
By right of mind, to exercise free-thought ;

To think, to act, or not, as each might choose,*
While charity and sympathy would make
The rule of life, and education thence
A duty, forced on all the sons of men ;
While science demonstrates the truth and power
Of that great law, which proves the brain
The source of mental force, and gives each faculty
Its separate organ, varying forms
Of size and quality, each with its own
Just means of satisfaction.   Thus the brain
Becomes as readable as other forms
Throughout the visible, wide universe.
Thus, hand in hand, throughout the whole of life,
Go form, capacity, and character.
Mind thus explained, make motives plain to sense,
And drive away the mystic clouds from truth.

    Our friend, so gentle, noble, true, and good,
Was aye—with brain and pen—among the brave
Who strove to bring both peace and plenty too,
To all the world, by sharing in results
With social justice ; working each for all,
On lands well tilled, made bright with teeming corn,
Where now these blessings of the earth are held
By sordid, 'centage-grabbing millionaires,
Who neither toil nor spin, yet live at ease,
In gross luxurious idleness, on labour's fruits—
On wealth now made by other hands than theirs.
He saw and felt this wrong to working men,
And sought to banish competition, war—
Where waste and want make desolate the world.

    Who would not help that happy day to come,
When labour's fruits enriching all mankind ;
Where all could aid to make a paradise
Of truth and beauty, blessing all who know
The forces nature yields for common use ?

---

* See " Freewill and Law," " Moral Freedom Reconciled with Causation," by
Dr. Travis ; published by Longmans and Co., Paternoster-row, London.

In past long ages, selfish egotism
Has seen a sensuous, wasteful revelry
The aim of life, among the ruling few,
With gnawing want and sorrow for the poor.
But knowledge yet shall make men free.　Mankind
Will see a change of front in days to come,
When social truths shall make a brotherhood,
And peoples, nations, races dwell in peace,
And bless the names of social pioneers,
While Travis points the way that all should go.

E. T. CRAIG.

(From a Photograph taken at Eighty Years of Age.)

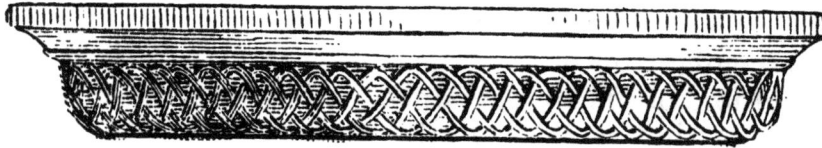

Memoir of E. T. Craig,

*One of the Originators of the Co-operative Movement,
Founder and Historian of Ralahine.*

SOCIAL Pioneers and men of original thought seldom live long enough to see the realisation of their views, or the proximate success of their sanguine hopes as to their plans, when their proposals are in direct opposition to the existing conditions of society, and in advance of the opinions of the age. The life of Mr. Craig has been a very long and very active one in promoting social amelioration, and in aiding human progress. Having lived to four score years, he now enjoys the rare satisfaction of seeing some of the plans he advocated and helped to organise in early life in a condition of extraordinary and unexampled prosperity, and mainly through the system of combined and organised action which his prompting suggestiveness advised, more than half a century ago.

The events of Mr. Craig's career are mostly embodied in the work he has achieved, some account of which is given in an interesting autobiographic record in an American journal, a memoir recently published in the *Phrenological Magazine*, and in his published works, such as the *History of Ralahine*, and in his active connection with the origin and organisation of the coöperative movement. From these sources we find that Mr. Craig has passed through a very varied, active, useful, and chequered career. Born in Manchester on August 4th, 1804, and losing his father at four years of age, he was sent to his paternal grandparents at Lancaster. His first impressions of social and political life were awakened by the war fever which raged in his family, one of his uncles being a militia man preparing to receive Napoleon and his army on their threatened invasion of England, and the trials and execution of the Luddites of Lancashire. His grandfather, a descendant of one of the followers of the Stuarts, who in the rebellion of 1745 remained and settled as a farmer at Milnthorpe, married a Miss Bell, whose sister held a post as custodian of the Courts of Law on the Civil side of Lancaster Castle, an office which had been held by members of her family for a period of a century, and they were of course, great admirers of the powers that be in Church and State. As a boy the subject of our story had free access to the Assize Courts, and soon became familiar with the faces and figures of the leading actors in those stirring times of the Radical Reformers, called Luddites : Henry Brougham, Scarlett, and Joe Nadin, the big, burly, bullet-headed constable of Manchester were well-known.

One of the awakenings to the realities of life was the frequent arrivals of coaches loaded with Luddites, guarded by dragoons with drawn swords, at the King's Arms Yard, near Mr. Craig's residence. The prisoners, chained together at their ankles and their hands, would be led out in a line, and sometimes in double lines of eight or ten, when they would march to the music of their manacles up the steep Castle Hill, where, with their pale faces and hollow eyes, they would, with a wild and bewildered gaze, get their first view of the dark, lofty towers, and massive gateway of John O'Gaunt's Castle, where many of them entered as their living tomb, departing life on the other side, strangled by the hangman's rope as a remedy for poverty and a cure for discontent. Often seven and eight at a time were thus throttled, to stifle for ever their cry of wretchedness or resistance to their oppressors. A few were condemned for incendiarism, having set fire to factories. Having, as was said, the free run of the courts and corridors, the charges against the poor starving weavers were soon discovered to be made chiefly by Nadin.* Mr. Craig often saw the wretched victims of ignorance, poverty, and injustice, after the sentence of death had been passed upon them, prepared by the parson to believe, at the last moment, that all the sins of their past life were forgiven and heaven was to be opened unto them by virtue of the hangman's hempen breviary. Among one batch was seen a boy about twelve years of age, who had been instigated by riotous weavers,

---

* The working men of Manchester for many years cherished an intensely bitter hatred of the memory of this unscrupulous instrument of the Tory magistrates. When his body, after death, was being removed for interment, a gentleman asked a working man, " Where are they going to take him ? " and he replied with strong feeling, " To hell, sir ! "

whom poverty held in an iron grasp with the shadow of the gallows ever before them, to set fire to a cotton mill at Wigan. When tied and pinioned ready for execution he began to cry most piteously for his mother, "Where's my mother? Oh! Where's my mother? My mother! My mother!" Evidently the young victim of society's cruel injustice was under the impression that his mother could release him from the hangsman's clutches.

On the death of his grandmother Mr. Craig returned to Manchester in time to enjoy the illuminations for the victory at Waterloo, and to see the misery, wretchedness, rioting, and destruction of machinery, as the supposed cause of the distress. In 1819 he was present at the Peterloo massacre, where 60,000 persons from various towns in Lancashire had marched, five abreast, with bands playing and banners flying, assembled to petition for the abolition of the Corn Laws, and for a Reform in Parliament. A relative, being a supervisor in the excise, was summoned to attend as a special constable. Two hundred of these were in a double line to form a passage from the platform to the house where the magistrates sat to regulate their proceedings. Mr. Craig saw the horrible scenes of massacre by the Manchester Yeomanry, where men, women, and children were slaughtered without the slightest pretext or sign of disorder. Eleven persons were killed and six hundred wounded, and mostly by sabre cuts. The only case of resistance he ever heard of was that by Joseph Smith, a plumber and glazier, who, on seeing one of the yeomanry cut down a woman with an infant in her arms, found a brick-bat and unhorsed the heartless and brutal butcher.† For several years the Reformers of Manchester assembled on the spot on the anniversary of the massacre, and sang a hymn, written for the occasion by Elijah Ridings.

About this time an accident arose from a boy throwing a piece of a broken plate at his brother, but which the air diverted from its object, and struck Mr. Craig near the temple. causing much loss of blood. Some passing strangers carried him to the infirmary, where the medical men bled him still more. However, in about a week he recovered so far as to enable him to wander among the various wards, where he saw the lancet often used in varying phases of disease, arising out of accidents to men in their

---

† Joseph Smith, after the Peterloo massacre, wore a white hat, the Radical Reformer's color and protest, and was therefore turned out of the Methodist Sunday School. He became a Socialist and an active pioneer in the Coöperative Sunday School and Educational Movement, and died recently at Maple Spring, on the Wissahickon, near Philadelphia, America.

employments. One or two amputations, the operating room being next to his own, awakened a deep interest in the structure and anatomy of the body, as the surgeons usually left the door open when Mr. Craig's boyish inquisitiveness led him to enter to look at the amputated limbs, which were left in their livid condition in pails of water kept ready to receive them.

These experiences gave a new aspect to the realities of life, and of human suffering among the producing classes. A short time after this accident Mr. Craig was put to the employment of fustian cutting. which was a profitable business till 1825, when reckless speculation prompted the manufacturers to over-production by multiplying apprentices, when wages were reduced to the lowest possible amount. The slaves of capital had no union, nor any resources, and the manufacturers, taking advantage of their weakness, reduced the wages of their work-people till they were often below one-half of what had been paid two years before.

Mr. Craig now began to learn from experience and observation the terrible lessons of uncontrolled selfishness and competition, in the system of unjust abatements, and the unscrupulous robbery of the fruits of the toil of the workmen in refusing to pay for more than five-sixths or six sevenths of the work done, while nominally paying what was due. Some of the manufacturers were viewed in these transactions as vultures feeding upon the hearts of the wage-slaves, or the chained Prometheus, justice. Enslaved by competition, the laborer had no choice but to accept the heartless terms of the capitalist employer or starve. This experience led Mr. Craig to a process of reasoning which resulted in holding and publicly advocating the principle that, as wealth is the result of labor, all working men should share in the profits arising from the sale or exchange of the fruits of their industry : a doctrine which he holds to the present day, and has seen successfully realized.

To the existence and influence of the Manchester Mechanics' Institution, established in 1825, with its large library, its lectures, and its classes, Mr. Craig acknowledges great obligations.

When with his family at Lancaster he was much indulged, and allowed to seek his own sources of amusement without constraint or direction, and was accustomed to amuse himself on the banks of the tidal river Lune in watching the movements of the fish, and the ships, then resorting to the port, but subsequently, from political motives removed to Liverpool. Although his friends were very loyal to Church and State, he was never required to attend either Sunday School or Church, and wandered through the rural lanes and districts to his heart's content and enjoyment of the healthful amusement. On his return to Manchester he found his mother's family rigid Calvanists, and he had to read aloud two chapters in Brown's Bible, and commentaries on each, and attend family prayers twice a day. To look out of the parlor window, or to whistle on a Sunday, was sinful. Reading scientific books was said to be using the instruments of Satan for the destruction of the human soul. The books selected from the library of the Mechanics' Institution were deemed so objectionable by his pious parents that he carried them in secret to his bedroom and there pursued his studies till two and three o'clock in the morning, with his pillow under his feet to avoid any disturbance or annoyance to his family in their bedroom below. The books, however, had the effect of leading him into an opposite view of believing that, while Sunday was then made the most dismal day in the week, it was the best adapted for the working classes to seek their own improvement by study and mental culture, and finding that the long hours of labor prevented his attendance at some of the classes at the Mechanics' Institution, he, with a few others, organised what was called the Utility Society, for the formation of classes and the delivery of lectures by the members on Sunday afternoons. This movement ended in the establishment of the celebrated Salford Sunday School and Social Institute. From one hundred to one hundred and fifty attended the school and classes, and several of the pupils afterwards became well-known as public lecturers and teachers.

Gratified with the results, Mr. Craig became active in promoting coöperation in the neighboring towns of Stockport, Oldham, Rochdale, Bury, etc. The societies were but few in number and not on sound principles. Some both bought and sold on credit, while the managers were poor book-keepers; others were badly managed and soon fell into confusion. Mr. Craig held then, as now, that credit is an evil, and that rent and interest should be abolished by cash payments. Seeing that the societies were getting into confusion, and that there was no controlling or guiding council, he advised the appointment of delegates from the various societies to form a congress, with power to frame regulations for the guidance of the societies. The first congress was held in Manchester in 1831, when, on the recommendation of Mr. Craig, systematic organisation and education was resolved upon. In the course of a short time a number of lecturers or coöperative missionaries were appointed to various districts, receiving weekly wages from a common fund. The first society which adopted the plan of a reading-room, classes, lectures, and a library was that of which he was president. The secretary was Mr. A. Heywood, ex-mayor of Manchester, who was imprisoned three months for selling unstamped newspapers. In 1831 the *Lancashire Coöperator* was published and Mr. Craig became its first editor.

Its object was " to expose to the workman's view a real picture of his situation, to awaken him to a sense of his powers when in unison with his fellows, to arouse him from his lethargy, like Hercules from his slumbers; not to deeds of violence, not to take from others that which they have already extracted from him, but in a bold, vigorous, and free inquiry into the causes of his mental and physical degradation, and to an investigation of the proposed remedy—coöperation—and the production of new wealth, hereafter, for his own use and benefit, by participating in the profits realised out of the sale or exchange of whatever he creates by his own labor."

In the same year he was invited to undertake the establishment of an Agricultural Coöperative Farm at Ralahine, County Clare, Ireland. At that time the population in the South of Ireland was in a state of wild insurrection and turbulence. Owing to the effects of the famine and the evictions by the landlords, agrarian outrages, and murders were numerous. The Steward at Ralahine was shot in the presence of his wife, and the landlord had to remove his family for safety. He applied to parties to help him to subdue the disorder, but none could or would aid him. He came to England and was advised to apply to Mr. Craig. After some little hesitation and stipulation as to sharing profits, if any, with labor after the rent was paid, he consented, and, at the sacrifice of a legacy went, and met with great opposition, his life being threatened and his grave dug. Yet in three months the laborers were organised under the New System, and the Terry Alts became orderly, industrious, contented, and comfortable, to the surprise of everybody. Mr. Craig has written the *History of Ralahine*, published by Trubner and Co. The story is translated into Italian, French, and German languages. The work is spoken of as " a romance of facts and figures." A London daily paper considers the book as " an historical romance that supplies a lesson which may yet benefit the whole world."

The system of sharing profits with the laborers was imitated with success on 100 acres in County Galway upon the system adopted by Mr. Craig at Ralahine.

For more than fifty years Mr. Craig has advocated the system of participation in management and sharing profits with producers or laborers, and the example he set has been followed with the happiest results both in France, Germany, and America. He contends that a duly regulated system of participation of management and sharing of profits would prove, not only of vast benefit to the workman, but also a great boon to the capitalist as an employer. The beneficial results of the system of labor upon profits are exerted in three ways: by increasing the quantity, improving the quality, and diminishing the cost of production. The system was introduced into Germany in 1847, and has been continued on the estate at Tellow, near Tetrow, during three generations of landlords, with the greatest success and satisfaction to all parties. A similar experiment was carried on at Bredow after 1872, with marked success. The laborers received in 1873-4 and 5, on an average, sums equal to £58 18s., while the average annual wages of agricultural laborers in the German empire, according to Professor von Goltz, is only £33 4s.

The most complete and brilliant example of the benefits of participation are illustrated by the Familistère, established by M. Godin, of Guise, where the benefits are seen in relation to education, sanitary measures, and social arrangements. These facts clearly demonstrate that in the system of participation and organization we have the means of effecting, without violence, a great social revolution in the relations of labor to capital.

Many visitors were attracted to Ralahine by the novelty of a set of turbulent agitators and discontented (because unemployed) Terry Alts being transformed by the system of participation into orderly, industrious laborers, paying £900 a-year for the rent and interest of 618 acres, with buildings and stock. The people built their own dwellings, and by a committee regulated the whole establishment with a success that awakened the surprise of all who saw the change. At the time of Mr. Craig's arrival the whole of the county was at the mercy of the famishing laborers. In the immediate neighbourhood of Ralahine there were four murders in the first six weeks after his arrival, and the violence of the agrarian outrages caused the district to be described as " hell upon earth !" Within a few months all was changed, both in the county and the province of Munster, while other counties required the suspension of the *Habeas Corpus Act* and Coercion Bills to control them. The system came to an end through no default of the people or the plan, but through the pecuniary obligations of the landlord. The people were evicted without the slightest regard to the value of their improvements, and the twenty acres added to the tillage land of the estate.

On leaving Ralahine Mr. Craig was invited by Lady Noel Byron to organise an industrial, mechanical, and agricultural school at Ealing, near London, where he originated a system in which industry in the garden or the workshop alternated with intellectual culture, with the best results, mentally and morally, to the pupils. Mr. Craig in the interim visited the industrial schools in Holland and Switzerland, and became a resident for three months at Hofwyl, the admirable institution of E. de Fellenberg, the pioneer of industrial training.

The Ealing Grove Agricultural School was established in 1834, and was so successful that it became a show-place to the aristocracy, and visitors had to be limited to one day in the week. Among others were Ada Byron and Lord King, to whom she was afterwards married; the Duchess of Roxburgh, Lady Lytton Bulwer, Mrs. Somerville, and Sir John K. Shuttleworth, Secretary to the Privy Council of Education, who, in his evidence before a Select Committee of the House of Commons, said:—"I think no one can fail to observe, on entering a school conducted upon that plan (originated by Mr. Craig), that there is a more kindly relation between the children and each other, and that there is an absence of that jealousy and personal irritation which is so frequently witnessed; that the children are more prone to kind offices towards each other and towards the master, and that they are breathing a purer and superior moral atmosphere than in a school which is conducted upon the ordinary system." The plan led the way to the industrial and reformatory schools now so successfully supported by the government.

Mr. Craig holds that those who cannot educate the young without corporal punishment do not understand the materials they undertake to mould and modify; they do not comprehend the knowledge, nature or spirit essential to successful training of the human faculties. Great and surprising success was realized by his method, which discarded corporal punishments, place-taking, and prizes. Both in industry and intellectual progress highly satisfactory results were attained.

So fond were the boys of their school that they would climb over the boundary walls before school hours to get at their gardens or to feed their rabbits. The village school, conducted by a nephew of the parish clerk, was deserted by the boys for the industrial school, and the schoolmaster, who was crippled in one hand, and often used the cane with the other, was under the necessity of appealing to his friends for aid. He wrote a letter to Lady Byron, showing that the industrial school had ruined his school, and her ladyship, with the usual waywardness of her charity, put the poor failing schoolmaster into Mr. Craig's position; and the young men he had trained as teachers had to give him the benefit of our friend's experience and methods of training!

About this time the son-in-law of Dr. Southwell Smith applied to Robert Owen for an introduction to the best practical educator he knew, and the founder of the celebrated New Lanark Schools took Mr. Hill to the residence of Mr. Craig, who became the editor of the *Star in the East*, in 1836. This was the first weekly newspaper devoted to the advocacy of co-operation and English Socialism.* He established a successful educational movement in Wisbeach, which led to an advanced system of education in art, science, and natural philosophy, forming what may be termed a Lady's College.

Owing to unwise speculations in the corn trade, the proprietor became bankrupt, when Mr. Craig was again socially shipwrecked and penniless, and obliged to rely on his own independent energies. Mr. Hill repeatedly applied to him to aid in new educational speculations; but his experience of Mr. Hill's self-seeking disposition, united to his inability to appreciate the work of those who had made repeated sacrifices to promote his aims, caused Mr. Craig to decline his invitations, and thenceforward, during sixteen years, he devoted himself to the profession of public lecturer on phrenology, co-operation, psychology, and kindred subjects. He visited nearly every town in England. During this period a great change for the worse had taken place in the co-operative movement. Congresses had not been held for some years; many societies had ceased to exist owing to adverse circumstance; the missionary lecturers had long since discontinued their labours, while the socialising influences seemed to be dying out. The Beer Bill was a great temptation to some stores. A beer-house, called " The Co-operator," was licensed next door to a very flourishing store at Northampton. But the society fell to pieces. Mr. Craig successfully opposed the movement which aimed at making the store an agent in the distribution of beer.

* English Socialism differs from Continental Socialism in advocating social ameliorations by the peaceful methods of reason and argument in opposition to force or violence.

Eventually, he was compelled to relinquish his efforts as a lecturer, owing to the health of Mrs. Craig.

While lecturing on phrenology and kindred subjects Mr. Craig's attention was attracted to the strange phenomena connected with animal magnetism, and as there seemed a possibility of its solving certain mental phenomena, he began assiduously to investigate its principles, and although he failed to satisfy himself as to the truth of much that was claimed on its behalf, he admitted the possibility of thought-reading, or of the transmission of mental impressions, and gave some remarkable expositions in Edinburgh, to which city he was invited by Mr. George Combe and Mr. James Simpson, the writer on education. He had two committees formed for the investigation of his methods. One was composed principally of literary men, and included such men as Professor Wilson, the Messrs. Chambers, George Combe, etc. The committee met at the house of Mrs. Crowe, author of the " Nightside of Nature." Various experiments were made, and in one case to demonstrate the important fact that the function of the nerves of feeling could be suspended, so that painless surgical operations could be performed. A young man was rendered insensible to feeling, and in that state a double tooth was extracted by Mr. Robert Nasmyth, Surgeon-Dentist to the Queen. The subject showed not the slightest sign of feeling. Mr. Craig was afterwards informed that Dr. Simpson had adopted his methods with certain patients ; subsequently, as is well known, he applied chloroform for the same purpose, and was made a baronet in consequence. Mr. Craig's experiments called forth so much opposition and misrepresentation that he felt compelled to issue a monthly journal, entitled *The Annals of Mesmerism*, in which some of his demonstrations are recorded.

In 1858 Mr. Craig again became associated with journalism, as Editor of the *Leamington Advertiser*. Subsequently he established the *Brighton Times* for the proprietor, and also edited the *County Express*. While Editor of the *Oxford University Herald* he determined to direct public attention to his discovery and plans for perfect ventilation. He had also directed his attention to sanitary requirements and as he publicly opposed the double system of drainage, he devised the ash-closet. He held that the rainfall should never be mixed with the sewage. The first should go to the river, and the last to the soil. Owing to the heavy charges for patents, Mr. Craig's plans were stolen or pirated. The first was stolen by a man who had requested Mr. Craig to accept him as a partner to push the sale of the invention. Not inclined to accept him, he induced a mutual friend at Manchester to visit Mr. Craig in Oxford. He requested to see his plans. In less than three months after, the Ash-closet was sold for £300 to the Shaftesbury Park Estate, as a patent invention of the vendors. An improvement was made upon the first plan and shown to the Members of the Coöperative Central Board in Manchester. Among them was a servant employed by the Manchester Corporation. He was gratified by the invention and recommended Mr. Craig to make the plan known by public lectures. Before there was time to complete arrangements for a lecture, Mr. W——— had got a joiner in Hulme to apply the plan to the Ash-middens of Manchester, and then induced the Sanitary Committee to adopt the system as his invention, to the exclusion of others. This was done, and many thousands of pounds per annum have been expended upon the application of the plan. The pirate was looked upon as a "genius" by some, and his wages raised from a small sum to £300 a year which he has since enjoyed, while Mr. Craig has lost his labor, his skill, and his money, without any compensation. Seeing the defective condition in the structure of dwellings, Mr. Craig devised several methods for Sanitary improvements. At an Exhibition of Arts and Manufactures in 1873, he was awarded the first prize, a Silver Medal, for the greatest number of useful inventions. Among the number was a fire-escape, which a man named Hill pirated, and actually exhibited before Capt. Palin, the Superintendent of the Manchester Police. The exhibition took place in the Police Yard in Albert Square. Mr. Craig has, we believe, inventions not yet made known, as his health gave way from bronchitis, caused by his labors in ventilation. As the Editor of the *Phrenological Magazine* remarks with some truth, Mr. Craig "seems to have been one of those ' geniuses ' who can do anything better than make money. It would take a volume to recount all Mr. Craig's useful and philanthropic labors." Amid all his pre-occupations, however, he never lost sight of his first love, Mutual Coöperation. In 1860 it was again in a low condition. No Congresses were held ; in 1866-7 he suggested the organization of a Central Board, Annual Congresses, with papers and Exhibitions of Manufactures. Since that day the progress of Coöperation has been one continued success of the most marvellous character, although it has not yet reached the essential point of combined funds as capital for productive purposes on the land, as was anticipated.

Mr. Craig has directed attention to other departments of political action, and was instrumental in improving the Irish Land Bill after it had passed the third reading. No provision had been made regarding the agricultural laborer, who was the chief cause of discontent and disturbance. In renting con-acre ground from farmers the laborers were robbed by their employers, as they were required to pay from five to eight pounds sterling for permission to occupy the ground with potatoes, for which the farmers paid only 15s. or £1 an acre. Mr. Craig showed that much labor and time was lost by the distance the laborers had daily to walk. He proposed to put the laborers' claims for half an acre, a cottage and rent for con-acre under the Land Court. This is now the law ; unfortunately it is only permissive. It is, however, a great boon to the laborers where it is in action.

To Mr. Craig is due the opposition made against the proposal, in accordance with the wishes of the late Prince Albert, for removing the National Gallery from Trafalgar Square to Kensington Gore, so that the Royal Academy might have the sole possession of the National property. Mr. Craig opposed the movement on the ground of the loss it would be to the people visiting the metropolis as well as to the working classes of London. The Royal Academy had to find its new quarters at Burlington House. When it was proposed to erect an obelisk of granite, which had been selected as a monument, Mr. Craig published a pamphlet condemning it as wanting in the elements necessary to awaken sympathy, and suggested the sculptured forms of Philosphers, Poets, Sculptors, Architects and Statesmen for the base of the monument, as seen in Hyde Park ; which makes it one of the most interesting monumental memorials in the world.

Mr. Craig is the author of several works on Phrenology, Shakespere, Art and Genius ; the Currency, Work and Wages ; and on Participation in Profits ; about which he still retains his faith, as on every envelope of his letters he has the following :—

WEALTH IS CREATED BY LABOR,
AND EVERY WORKMAN
SHOULD SHARE IN THE PROFITS
ARISING FROM THE EXCHANGE OR SALE
OF THE FRUITS OF HIS INDUSTRY.

We have said little of Mr. Craig's leading mental characteristics, having spoken mainly of his work. We may, however, close our record with the remarks of the *Phrenological Magazine* when speaking of his mental and moral tendencies as indicated by his photographic portraits :—

" His natural refinement, taste, and imagination, with large Language, qualify him to express himself in a free, easy, graceful style, enabling him to present many unpleasant truths in a pleasing and acceptable manner. The moral brain, especially Benevolence, is largely represented, which disposes him to take an interest in the welfare of mankind at large, but especially in that of the more dependent class. He has great firmness and tenacity of purpose, and is quite decided in purpose, tenacious in his plans, systematic in his arrangements, and methodical in his life and habits."

It is gratifying to know that Mr. Craig is still contributing to aid in the progress of Liberal movements in Social Reform. On the 11th July, 1883, Mr. and Mrs. E. T. Craig, (born Aug. 4th 1804, and July 15th 1810) greeted their Friends on the Fiftieth Anniversary of their Happy Union and Golden Wedding Day.

The following lines were inscribed under the Portrait of Mrs. Craig on that Anniversary :—

FULL FIFTY YEARS of happy life
Have seen thee maiden, mother, wife.
When first I met thee, warm and young,
I found thee fair, with tuneful tongue
Which won my heart's responsive sigh,
And made me seek thee ev'ry joy.
Our mutual trust made mutual love,
Nor needed cleric aid to prove
That Constancy may live and reign
In hearts that seek the Truth to gain.
We pledged our troth to each, I ween,
Before we reached our Ralaheen.
There life was one sweet round of joy,
That never felt or feared alloy.
Too soon we learnt the world's cold heart,
But never shrank from duty's part.
Thy sensibility had fears,
While grief would often end in tears ;
My words would wound without intent,
Till fuller speech made clear how meant.
And oft my eager pen would paint
The wrongs in Labor's bitter plaint.
With damning words of keenest tone,
Till thy sweet voice would softly moan

And counsel peace with tuneful chords
Of Charity and gentle words.
Hence many a caustic, biting phrase
Has passed away in milder phase.
Though mutual trust brought mutual joy—
The source of ev'ry social tie—
We soon must reach th' untrodden shore,
Whence never mortal came before,
To tell the secrets still unknown
Of Pain or Bliss at Mercy's throne.
What though no weeping friends appear
To grieve by rule— wear weeds a year ?
What though nought black our ashes grace,
" Or marble emulate thy face ?"
What though no sacred earth have room,
Nor solemn dirge be sung with gloom ?
Thy grave with living flow'rs shall glow,
And sweet moss roses yearly blow,
While larks shall trill thy requiem high,
And birds join chorus in the sky.
We've tried to make a happier world
By Love and Duty's flag unfurled ;
We've lived our lives of love full well,
And, joyful, soon must say—" FAREWELL !"

Mutual Exchanges are impeded, and often retarded, by any fluctuating Medium, which is made to rule the discounts, to the injury of the Farmer, the Tradesman, the Manufacturer, and the Laborer.

The Irish Land and Labor Question

AND

HISTORY OF RALAHINE.

By E. T. CRAIG.

TRUBNER & CO., LUDGATE HILL; W. REEVES, 185, FLEET STREET, LONDON.

With Portraits of the Author, Fellenberg, Lady Byron, &c. 8vo, 204 pages, price 2s. Bound and lettered, 2s. 6d.

"It is an industrial romance that supplies a lesson which may yet benefit the whole world."—*Daily Chronicle.*

"The arrangements were in most respects admirable, and reflected the greatest credit upon Mr. Craig, as an organiser and administrator. To his wisdom, energy, tact, and forbearance the success of the experiment was due."—*Mark Lane Express.*

"The book is full of valuable advice, and of the records of a rich experience."—*Lloyds' Weekly Newspaper.*

"If ever there was a romance in facts and figures, it is the story of Ralahine—a fairy tale of political economy, by one who had been an eye-witness of its reality."—*Spectator.*

"Its effect on the laborers was immense. Every man worked with a will, outrage ceased, and the most kindly feelings prevailed; in fact, the whole country felt the soothing effect of a system which showed the laborer the way to practical independence, and induced in him the content and satisfaction of prosperity."—*Observer.*

WORKS BY THE SAME AUTHOR.

SHAKSPERE, ART, AND THE HERITAGE OF GENIUS. Second Edition. Per post, 2s. 6d.

"I owe you many thanks for your very elegant, learned, and important disquisition on the Mask and Portraits of Shakspere."—*C. Holt Bracebridge, Hon. Secretary to the Shakspere House Committee.*

WORK AND WAGES; OR, CAPITAL, CURRENCY, AND PRODUCTION. Second Edition. Per post, 6d.

"Mr. Craig entertains sound views, and, possessing great power of expression, he has produced a most telling work."—*The "Citizen," a Banking Journal.*

HAND LABOUR AND HEAD WORK; OR, INDUSTRIAL TRAINING. Per post, 6d.

www.ingramcontent.com/pod-product-compliance
Lightning Source LLC
Chambersburg PA
CBHW081306040426
42452CB00014B/2671